Critical Acclaim
How a Blog Held Off the Most Powerful Union in America

This is an exceptional overview of the importance of social media as a means to meet the challenge of a corporate campaign directly and effectively. These campaigns are designed to drive reckless accusations far and wide with the hope of no counter argument. Levy clearly demonstrates that blogs and social media outlets provide the immediacy of a response that can neutralize the bold and often unsubstantiated claims employed by unions during these onslaughts.

Vin Petrini
Senior Vice President of Public Affairs
Yale New Haven Health System

SEIU is masterful at using the language and imagery of civil rights and social justice to tap the values and emotions of employees, clergy, educators, and elected officials. Discussing the union's playbook *and* being able to counter its effectiveness was a notable accomplishment. Levy's own values and imagery are consistent with liberal tradition, lending his explanations and his arguments particular weight. He established a position of credibility and addressed the issues without legalese.

His blog created a real-time forum for his hospital's community. This had the effect of making visible comments by stakeholders that would otherwise have been privately expressed, if at all. This virtual public square buttressed his position and established his viewpoint as legitimate, if not normative.

    Thomas P. Quinn
    Past President & CEO, Community General Hospital, Syracuse, NY

Just as we have seen Arab Spring erupt from chaos because of the use of new forms of social media, and Ai Weiwei thwart the Chinese government with his use of the internet to spread his freedom message, Paul Levy's effective use of the blogosphere to frame and advance his side of a union-management conflict illustrates how leaders can use social media effectively in a modern era of health care and business.

Levy artfully tells the story of getting his hospital's message out without having a war chest to spend on public relations. His persistent and effective use of social media evened the playing field and allowed him to keep diverse audiences informed and engaged.

    Harris A. Berman, M.D.
    Boston

What a fascinating story! This is a powerful lesson in winning a battle of perception with the modern tools of transparency and internet speed.

Roni Zeiger MD
CEO, Smart Patients

Paul Levy, an innovative, caring, thoughtful, and strategic hospital CEO, writes convincingly how he used a blog, a low cost vehicle, to help counter a well-financed union corporate campaign that sought a neutrality agreement and card check. The blog communicates effectively with several important audiences – the trustees, the staff, the doctors, the media, the Jewish community, and the general public. This fascinating story deserves to be read, it offers lots of insights and useful lessons.

Fred K. Foulkes
Professor of Organizational Behavior
Boston University

You have put forth an accurate portrayal of the strategy and tactics of the SEIU "playbook", as well as the BIDMC moves to level the playing field under your leadership. Importantly, you have also displayed your keen understanding of the intersection of policy, politics and communications--and the use of social media to navigate those treacherous paths. The rejection of a "traditional" media strategy was critical to your success.

As a longtime advocate in the public arena, I know how important it is to "frame" an issue. The research you did, and the execution of your own game plan, put the union on its heels with its baseless efforts to portray you as anti-union. You were always in front of the issue with the "click of a button". You intuitively understood your constituencies and fended off potential adversaries while securing important allies. You epitomized the old adage that "everyone is entitled to an opinion, but not your own set of facts."

> **Bob Gibbons**
> **Recently retired long-time senior health care association executive and public servant**

A compelling demonstration of how a thoughtful CEO's blog can be an effective tool to provide organizational transparency, preserve the democratic process and ensure a level playing field for management and labor.

> **Marjorie Arons-Barron, strategic communications consultant, blogger and former editorial director of WCVB-TV, Boston**

Paul Levy shows how an open and honest dialogue using the tools of real-time online communications beats entrenched powers who play by the old rules of command and control. This isn't mere academic theory, it is a real business case in which Paul shares each twist and turn of the remarkable success of his unlikely David vs. Goliath battle.

> **David Meerman Scott, bestselling author of** *The New Rules of Marketing and PR,* **now in over 25 languages from Bulgarian to Vietnamese**

Corporate campaigns by unions seek to bypass secret ballot elections that are provided for workers under current law. It was the genius of Paul Levy to capitalize on that anti-democratic deficiency in the union's approach by shining the full light of exposure on this tactic. Supreme Court Justice Louis Brandeis said that "Sunlight is said to be the best of disinfectants" and Paul's use of social media and his blog was just the disinfectant needed to show a curious public that SEIU's campaign against Beth Israel Deaconess was no public service, but a frequently outrageous effort at self-promotion and union organizing without having to do the actual hard work of persuading employees to vote that a union was truly in the workers' interest. As the former head of the Illinois Hospital Association I was a front-line participant in spreading our own brand of sunshine over the darkness of SEIU and AFSCME's unsuccessful campaigns against some of our most dedicated faith based healthcare systems.

    Kenneth C. Robbins, JD
    President
    Illinois Hospital Association (1983-2009)

How a Blog Held Off

The Most Powerful Union

in America

Paul F. Levy

Copyright © 2013 Paul F. Levy.

All rights reserved. No part of this book may be reproduced or transmitted in any form or by any means electronic or mechanical, including photo copying, recording or by any information storage and retrieval system without written permission from the author, except for the inclusion of brief quotations in a review.

ISBN-13: 978-1482730777

Never, "for the sake of peace and quiet,"
deny your own experience or convictions.

Dag Hammarskjöld, *Markings*

Foreword

In this book, Paul Levy offers a compelling historical narrative of labor-management relationships over a tumultuous five-year period. While the story itself is riveting and the stakes compelling, it is more than simple case narrative; rather it is a morality play about an attempt at power dominance which, if realized, would have foreclosed employee engagement. Through such tactics as "neutrality agreements" and "card checks," a powerful union sought to become hostage-taker of a hospital's financial and reputational halo. Levy knew such an approach would usurp the primary goal of the hospital to preserve and enhance patient care. It would also deny employees the right to debate and determine the environmental parameters within which they worked. Thus the principles in play were no less than institutional purpose and individual prerogative.

To safeguard the sanctity of these principles, a communications strategy became key; Levy seized upon the beauty of the blog. Quite novel as a weapon in 2006, this social medium offered several advantages. First, Levy could move with dispatch, unfettered by the ponderous process and political predispositions of traditional newspapers. Not only was this vehicle flexible but it was frugal. Replete union coffers could subsidize advertising campaigns, but hospital funds had to serve the grander purpose of protecting patient care. Finally, with Levy at the helm, the blog could assimilate the views of employees and allow them a voice in forging their own destiny. They could assume the offense rather than wilting under the unremitting pressure of an outside party. By establishing links in the blog, Levy was able to frame the debate within a context of historical accuracy.

The result was victory for the hospital whose fundamental aspirations never fell victim to an external force. Levy writes with candor and persuasively elucidates a story whose dynamics can be replicated in other professional arenas. The book remains more, though, than a treatise on unions and those they seek to organize. Rather it is a passionate plea that process be predicated on mutual respect. By shortcutting process, any group will nullify the ethical validity of its intended outcome. Moreover, by failing to heed Levy's counsel about debate and disclosure, an interloper invites failure in the quest to create internal dissent and instead incurs backlash for the attack.

David P. Boyd
Professor of Management at Northeastern University
Former Dean of the Northeastern University Business School

Table of Contents

Foreword i

Author's Note v

About Corporate Campaigns 1

   Introduction 1

   The union's goal: Manipulate the balance of power in an organizing campaign 3

   Attack the company and degrade management's options 7

   SEIU: Experienced practitioner of corporate campaigns 9

   The key to a successful corporate campaign: Communicate wide, far, and hard 16

Mounting an effective counter-campaign 21

   The need to turn the tables 21

   Overall Strategy: Expose the playbook 27

Fronts in the War 35

   The first battlefield: Neutralize use of the religion card 35

   The second battlefield: Keep the doctors on board 46

   The third battlefield: Engage the staff 54

   The fourth battlefield: Engage and reassure the affiliate 60

   The fifth battlefield: Involve the governing bodies 63

   The sixth battlefield: Convey the story to the state legislature and Congress 66

   On the personal side: Prepare for the downside of speaking out 68

The result: A successful counter-campaign 73

Endnotes 77

Author's Note

There doubtless will be readers of this book who will try to portray it and me as anti-union. Nothing could be further from the truth. This book is about a struggle to maintain the rights of workers in the face of a union that sought to abrogate those rights. While unionizing would have created different dynamics and new challenges for management, the struggle was always about worker's rights more than unionization *per se.*

I have had a long and positive relationship with many unions during my career. For example, while Executive Director of the Massachusetts Water Resources Authority, I signed the largest project labor agreement in the history of the state, providing work rules for a unionized labor force on the multi-billion dollar Boston Harbor Cleanup Project. During that time and previously, as Chairman of the Massachusetts Department of Public Utilities, I always had a cordial relationship with the various state employees' unions. Likewise, when I was Administrative Dean at Harvard Medical School, I enjoyed an extremely friendly and helpful relationship with the Harvard Union of Clerical and Technical Workers. When I resigned from that post, they gave me a copy of the book describing their organizing history, *We Can't Eat Prestige,* inscribed with warm wishes from their members.

CHAPTER 1

About Corporate Campaigns

Introduction

On August 31, 2005, a front page story appeared above the fold in the *Boston Globe*: "A powerful New York healthcare union with a $20 million annual organizing budget and a quarter of a million members is poised to merge with a Boston local and intends to launch a major organizing drive at the city's top teaching hospitals."[i] Among the prime targets of this organizing effort was Beth Israel Deaconess Medical Center, the hospital of which I had become CEO in 2002.

This was an alarming development. BIDMC had just passed through tumultuous times resulting from a disruptive merger between Beth Israel Hospital and New England Deaconess Hospital. Annual operating deficits between 1996 and 2002 ranged from $40 million to $70 million, and the institution's balance sheet had diminished by 40 percent. By 2005, we had recovered from the annual deficits through a successful turnaround, but we were left in a weakened financial condition. There was no way that we could match a union's multimillion-dollar expenditure in an organizing drive and continue to meet our public service obligations to the community. But giving in to an organizing campaign that could lead to the introduction of prescriptive work rules for our service employees[ii] could also set back the hospital's strategy to be innovative and flexible in delivering the highest quality care to our patients.

Why should we have been worried, though? After all, the long-term decline in private sector unions in America had been well documented. From almost 25 percent of the workforce in 1973, the rate of unionization had fallen to under 8 percent in 2005.[iii] The trouble was that this trend came with a price tag. Among the major reasons for the decline in unions was the ability of corporations to run effective but costly counter-campaigns when unions sought to achieve representation through the organizing process. As mentioned, we did not have the resources to engage in an expensive battle.

More significantly, some unions had been able to buck this trend, most notably the 2.1 million-member national Service Employees International Union (SEIU), the one on its way to Boston. The SEIU had shown itself to be highly effective at wielding something called a "corporate campaign," which changed the dynamic of the organizing process. The corporate campaign attacks the reputation of the company being organized in an aim to weaken its position in the marketplace and disturb its relationship with key constituencies in the community. Faced with financial and reputation risk pressure, the corporation loses its resolve and concedes to significant changes to the normal organizing process that give the union the upper hand and a much higher probability of success. Meanwhile, patients, supporters, and other stakeholders are made to worry unnecessarily and are often brought into the fray.

The SEIU's former president, Andrew Stern, was reported to say, "We use the power of persuasion first. If it doesn't work, we try the persuasion of power."[iv] The targets of these corporate campaigns frequently find themselves on the defensive against public response and are often flummoxed by the intensity and thoroughness of the SEIU's efforts.

There is, however, a new arrow in the quiver for firms that are being attacked in a corporate campaign. Social media offers an effective remedy, if used early, thoughtfully, and decisively. This book tells the tale of one such counter-campaign, a story of how one blog held off the most powerful union in America.

The union's goal: Manipulate the balance of power in an organizing campaign

The history of labor negotiations is replete with stories and analyses of the relative bargaining power of unions and management during contract negotiations. Our story here, though, is about the interplay of relative power during the organizing process itself. Under traditional National Labor Relations Act (NLRA) rules, the aspiring union collects authorization cards signed by staff members who would constitute the bargaining unit. When thirty percent of employees have signed the cards, the union submits a petition to the National Labor Relations Board (NLRB) to schedule an election. A formal campaign for "yes" and "no" votes ensues, followed some time later by a binding secret ballot election. The results of that election determine whether all members of the relevant job classification are to be represented collectively by the union, or whether the prior non-union structure will continue.

The question of who has more power to influence the results of this process has been hotly debated. Unions assert that the company has the ability to intimidate, cajole, or otherwise influence workers and delay the process and thereby exert disproportionate power. Companies assert that the union has more influence because of its ability to make unsubstantiated promises to workers, to reach them in their homes and elsewhere off campus, and to prevail in the court of public opinion.

Without reaching a conclusion to this question here, we can nonetheless summarize the interplay between labor and management during this organizing process: Both attempt to win the hearts and minds of the workers, with the goal of accruing enough "yes" or "no" votes to win.

More interesting, though, is the question of how the two sides can manipulate the structure of the process to make their party's desired outcome more likely. If I am management, I want a structure that gives me time and forums to weaken the union's assertions that it is a more honest and effective representative of the workers. If I am the union, I want the opposite, and my traditional approach, both before and after the NLRB schedules an election, is to have as fast a process as possible, so that I can make my claims to the workers without giving the company sufficient time to raise doubts among them.

Recently, some labor unions have sought to change the rules in order to dramatically decrease management's ability to mount a counterattack. One such approach is to persuade the company to sign a "neutrality agreement," under which all officers, managers, supervisors, or agents of the company are forbidden to say anything negative about unionization in general and about the specific union in particular. In addition, management may not rebut any of the union's assertions about the value it will bring to the workers. Indeed, supervisors are precluded even from responding to workers' questions about the union drive. Instead, managers are supplied with printed cards, which they hand to the workers, saying that the worker should get the answers from a union representative.

This happened in January of 2009 in Boston, when the Caritas Christi hospital system signed a neutrality agreement with the Service Employees International Union. If a worker asked a supervisor about the pending union recognition drive, the manager was required to say nothing and hand over a card with the following message:[v]

> The Management Team of this hospital and 1199SEIU agree that the question of whether workers should be represented by 1199SEIU is a question the workers should answer for themselves in a secret ballot election. The hospital has agreed that supervisors will not answer questions or express any further opinion on the issue of union representation.

As should be obvious, the likelihood of a union victory in this situation is dramatically enhanced. With no counter-arguments presented to workers, any doubts they might have about the efficacy of collective bargaining are virtually eliminated. Indeed, that is precisely what happened in this case, with an overwhelming majority voting "yes."[vi]

An even more one-sided approach is the substitution of a "card-check" form of organizing and certification. Recall that the normal NLRA process calls for a certification election after 30% of the workers in a bargaining unit sign authorization cards. Under the card-check approach, when 50% of the workers sign authorization cards, the union is deemed to be certified, with no election or further action whatsoever. Management has virtually no opportunity to offer counter arguments about the benefits of unionization because there is never an election campaign with arguments presented by both sides.

Further, by removing a secret ballot process, the union introduces an approach that is rife with the potential for peer pressure and intimidation.

Attack the company
and degrade management's options

While a neutrality agreement or card-check is not specifically prohibited under the NLRA, its use requires assent by the employer. Management's best alternative to such a negotiated agreement is the established NLRA process, under which the company has a relatively high likelihood of success in fending off the union. All else being equal, there are few circumstances in which it would be in the company's interests to accede to union demands for a neutrality agreement or a card-check process. So why would management choose this path?

The answer is that the union acts to degrade the management's alternatives to the point that the company feels it to be more in its interest to agree to a neutrality agreement or card-check than the usual NLRA process. Here is where the concept of a corporate campaign comes into play.

Professor Jarol B. Manheim, of George Washington University, in his book *The Death of a Thousand Cuts*, explains.[vii]

> Corporate campaigns attack the viability of essential relationships on which any corporation depends – relationships with its customers, shareholders, bankers, regulators – in summary, with all of its key stakeholders... They are inevitably constructed around a myth that the corporation is a social outlaw, and they are designed to appeal to an underlying popular distrust of a big business.
>
> The stakes in a corporate campaign are real economic goods. The public face of the campaign, which tends to be heavily symbolic in character, is but a mask. Behind it are vested interests competing either for direct economic advantage or for some measure of economic restructuring.

As the title of Manheim's book suggests, the object of the corporate campaign is to gradually make life so uncomfortable for the company among its key constituencies that it cries, "Uncle!" The company gives up its rights under the NLRA, knowing full well that the union is likely to win the organizing campaign. It views a loss as preferable to continued "death by a thousand cuts" on the regulatory, financial, and public relations fronts.

Often, the true target in such a campaign, more than the senior management, is the board of directors or board of trustees of the firm or institution. The members of these groups are people whose reputations in the community, and sometimes worldwide, are important. They do not want adverse publicity to jeopardize those reputations, and so they put pressure on the management to accede to the neutrality agreement or card-check process.

With practice and experience, a union can become a true expert in the use of corporate campaigns, enhancing its record in organizing campaigns. The SEIU provides us with the best example of such expertise.

SEIU: Experienced practitioner of corporate campaigns

The Service Employees International Union was an early practitioner of corporate campaigns. Indeed, Manheim notes that "as early as 1988, the union published its own how-to guide, the Corporate Campaign Manual."[viii] In recent years, the SEIU has become a major adherent to the use of corporate campaigns and in so doing has become the fastest growing and most powerful union in America. In a variety of health care settings across the country, the SEIU has used its prodigious financial resources[ix] to garner influence and support among elected officials during political campaigns, to conduct detailed research about the professional and lay leaders of hospitals, and to prepare and submit documented complaints to federal, state, and local regulatory agencies.

Richard Haugh documented the corporate campaign approach in a 2006 article in *Trustee Magazine*:[x]

> Ken Robbins had never seen a labor organizing effort like it: Instead of a traditional grassroots drive to recruit members, a union in Illinois launched a series of very public attacks to discredit and embarrass a hospital. The goal:

to pressure executives to stay out of the way as the union signed up nurses and other employees.

The tactics bewildered Robbins, president of the Illinois Hospital Association. Wasn't it self-defeating, he asked a union leader, to try to weaken an employer where you already represent a fair number of workers and hope to represent the rest?

"I've known the guy a long time; he's a very solid guy," Robbins says. "He just told me, 'Ken, I know it doesn't make sense, but it works.'"

The article continued:

"In states where unions haven't played a big role yet, a lot of CEOs really aren't aware of just how bad it can get," says Jan Emerson, vice president of external affairs for the California Hospital Association. "They may sort of be aware of what's going on around the country, but in terms of just how ugly it can get, they don't have any idea."

An SEIU official demurred:

"The industry calls that a corporate campaign. That's not what we think it is," says Mary Kay Henry, executive vice president of SEIU's hospital division. "When employers make a different choice and decide to waste precious health care dollars on fighting workers' decision to form a union, we just use all the relationships necessary to convince them to take the other path."

But another article by L.M. Sixel in the *Houston Chronicle* provided tactical details:[xi]

> [The SEIU Contract Campaign Manual] recommends hiring students to pose as researchers to get inside information against a corporate target; find unrelated regulatory complaints for legal and regulatory pressure; and search a variety of sources, from divorce records to membership in clubs that discriminate to links with unpopular politicians, to find incriminating details on company officials.
>
> "It may be a violation of blackmail and extortion laws to threaten management officials with release of 'dirt' about them if they don't settle a contract," according to the guide, "but there is no law against union members who are angry at their employer deciding to uncover and publicize factual information about individual managers."

Sutter Health in California faced a long-lasting corporate campaign, reporting:[xii]

> The leaders of Oakland-based SEIU United Healthcare Workers West have engineered a systematic, multi-faceted misinformation campaign against the organizations that comprise the not-for-profit Sutter Health network of hospitals and doctors. Many of SEIU United Healthcare Workers West's tactics are counter to the union's purported role of representing caregivers at Sutter affiliates and go against the best interest of patient care.
>
> Frustrated over its lack of success in attracting new union members through traditional organizing efforts, SEIU

United Healthcare Workers West tries in myriad ways to disrupt patient care and embarrass caregivers across our network. One union leader described this type of campaign as "death of a thousand cuts rather than a single blow."

The hospital system outlined the elements of the SEIU strategy, noting that the union had:

- Aggressively opposed many critical projects proposed by Sutter affiliates, including new medical campuses in San Carlos, Novato, Santa Cruz and Sacramento. Ironically, each of these facilities includes new, rigorous seismic safety standards to better protect patients and employees – including the union's own members.

- Called upon the State of California to revoke Sutter Health's tax-exempt status.

- Tried to stop Sutter Health from accessing the bond market to make repairs and improvements to a number of Sutter-affiliated hospitals. The union then sent news releases to discourage investors from buying the bonds.

- Sent letters to individuals who have donated money to Sutter-affiliated hospitals and urged them to not contribute.

- Forced the cancellation of a Sutter Delta Medical Center-sponsored community event intended to raise money for critical breast cancer diagnostic equipment.

- Spent hundreds of thousands of dollars to prevent Castro Valley's Eden Medical Center, Sonoma County Hospital, Oakland's Summit Medical Center and San Francisco's St. Luke's Hospital from joining the Sutter Health network. Affiliation with a health care system was critical to the continued operation of these hospitals and all remain open today, as more stable operations offering new programs and services.

- Mounted a publicity campaign to discourage leaders of a struggling sole community provider hospital (Del Puerto, July 1997) in the San Joaquin Valley from becoming part of Sutter Health. The hospital chose another system partner and was immediately closed down. The union took credit for helping to affect the decision, but kept quiet when the hospital closed.

We also see one of the tactics at work in this report by Tom Quinn, the president and CEO of Community General Hospital in Syracuse, NY:[xiii]

> Yesterday members of SEIU 1199 picketed my home. Interestingly, the picketing was not intended to influence me at Community General Hospital, where I am CEO. Instead, SEIU seeks to use me to pressure one of Community's employees who serves on the Board of Iroquois Nursing Home.
>
> Corporate campaigns employ the methods of community organizing, political action, and public relations, such as letter writing, telephone calls, picketing, and publicity. SEIU corporate campaigns target elected officials, as well

as candidates for office, and they involve outside organizations in an effort to bring additional pressure on the Board and management of a target organization – in this case, Iroquois Nursing Home.

The CEO of a New York City hospital told me about a meeting he had with a high-ranking SEIU official in 2006 with regard to a group of 320 workers the union wanted to organize. The organizer demanded that the hospital agree to card-check or sign a neutrality agreement. "If you don't," he told the CEO, "we will smear the reputation of your hospital, your medical school, and your trustees, and hold up your building permits."

My colleague knew that this was not an idle threat, as he had watched the SEIU in action at nearby Yale-New Haven Hospital. In 2004, the hospital had approved the construction of a $430 million cancer center at a medical complex. The *New Haven Register* reported that the center would "establish the hospital as a major force in cancer research and medical services, rivaling the Dana-Farber Cancer Institute in Boston and Memorial Sloan-Kettering in New York." It would also "allow the hospital to consolidate cancer services that are now located at six sites on its medical campus."[xiv]

"The proposed center would add 112 beds to the current 854-bed capacity of the hospital, expand operating rooms and radiology services and add a women's cancer center. It is expected to meet a 20 percent growth rate in patient demand in the coming decade."

The SEIU used the cancer center project as an opportunity to revive what had been an unsuccessful campaign to organize 1,800 workers at the hospital. Organizers from the SEIU brought together neighborhood groups and formed a coalition that held a rally demanding the hospital provide funding for the "community." It soon became evident that New Haven's mayor, whose gubernatorial campaign the SEIU endorsed earlier that year, was using his office to pressure the hospital to recognize the union and that a union vote was a condition of approval of the hospital's expansion. The *New Haven Register* commented:[xv]

> Saturday marked an entire year of inexcusable city delay in the approval of Yale-New Haven Hospital's application to construct a 14-story expansion that includes the consolidation of its scattered and overcrowded cancer treatment facilities. Rather than be an honest broker as he has been in contract negotiations with Yale University and its unions, John DeStefano Jr. has used his office to pressure the hospital to recognize a union that has tried since 1997 to organize workers there.
>
> The mayor, who stripped the hospital's constables of police powers in a dispute about union activities at the hospital, has made the holding of a union vote a condition of approval of the hospital's expansion. The Service Employees International Union has, in turn, proposed design changes like underground parking that would make the project prohibitively expensive.

In his run for the Democratic nomination as governor, DeStefano is the candidate of organized labor. Not only the SEIU but 27 other labor locals or statewide unions have endorsed his run. The price of that support can be seen in his administration's handling of the cancer center proposal. There is no end in sight to the protracted city approval process.

Although no other zone in the city has a building height restriction, the city has imposed a height restriction on the cancer center. The city has twice turned down a demolition permit so even preliminary work can begin.

The key to a successful corporate campaign: Communicate wide, far, and hard

A corporate campaign earns its power only if key constituencies are made to believe that the targeted corporation is a "bad citizen" —how it is violating rules, regulations, and community norms of behavior. To be effective, the message must be delivered through a variety of media, and it must be repeated enough to be established as "fact" in the eyes of those constituencies.

Manheim notes: [xvi]

> The most vital component of any corporate campaign is the planning and implementation of an effective communications strategy. The legal, legislative, regulatory, and other aspects of the campaign are important, but it is the communications strategy that binds these various constitu-

ent elements into a unified whole, drives their development, and ultimately carries the campaign to its target audiences, where it will either succeed or fail.

In some respects, the union is like any other advertiser, using the many avenues of traditional and, more recently, social media to reinforce its message. Instead of selling a consumer product, though, the union attempts to denigrate the reputation of the hospital and those running it. But the campaign relies not only on established media: It seeks to employ all forms of communication, including personal communications from its allies to its target audiences. Eventually, members of the board of trustees (usually lay volunteers with important business roles in the community) forcefully say to management, "Would you please get these guys off our back? They are ruining our hospital's reputation and my personal reputation. How bad can it be to give in a little on the organizing process?"

Whatever a hospital's financial resources to fight this kind of public campaign, they pale in comparison to the SEIU's. The union has millions of dollars from members' dues and hundreds of people at its disposal as it carries out a campaign against a single hospital. The issue is not only that the hospital does not have the financial resources to match the union: The management is busy in the multi-faceted task of running a hospital and caring for patients. In contrast, the SEIU only has one job and is able to focus on it with all its energy. As a former undersecretary of labor said to me, "You know, this is the only thing these folks have to do."

The union also has easy access to a vast public forum. The SEIU's stories – portrayed as good versus evil, big guy versus little guy, good care versus bad care – are beguiling fodder for the media. The hospital is thrown back on its heels each time such a story is released. It is difficult to be prepared for a persuasive rebuttal. Indeed, in some cases, rebuttal is legally impossible, such as where the union's criticisms relate to matters of patient care or treatment of personnel. There, strong federal and state privacy laws preclude release of confidential information. The hospital is forced into saying, "We are not permitted to comment on that." There is nothing like the impression of stonewalling to further whet the interest of the media in carrying the union's message through subsequent stories. A story that should at most run for one day is found to have "legs," appearing several days over.

There is an important irony here. The fact that such stories are part of a corporate campaign is usually not considered newsworthy. The details of union organizing strategies are abstruse and uninteresting to reporters and their readers. Sure, the newspaper story might mention that the hospital and the union are at odds with regard to organizing the hospital's workers; but it will seldom mention that the publication of the adverse press release by the union is part of a determined public campaign to put pressure on management to erode the employees' rights during the organizing process.

Month after month, year after year, the campaign continues. In the case of the Yale New Haven Hospital and the SEIU, for example, the corporate campaign lasted seven years. An indication of its strength was that city politicians joined up with the union, holding up building permits for a new cancer center. A neutrality agreement was finally signed, illustrating that, absent a countervailing force, management usually finds its position degraded and gives in, either by signing a neutrality agreement or, in the extreme case, agreeing to a card-check process.

CHAPTER 2

Mounting an effective counter-campaign

The need to turn the tables

I considered this likely dynamic in 2006, a few months after the SEIU announced that it was coming to Boston to organize the academic medical centers and named our hospital as a top candidate. We reviewed the experience of Yale New Haven Hospital and its multi-year battle,[xvii] and we studied the use of corporate campaigns elsewhere in the health care sector. Our senior leadership group quickly concluded that neutrality agreements or card-check forms of organizing were antithetical to the long-standing tradition of open discourse and debate in our hospital. We believed in democracy and the right of workers to determine their own future, and we felt that as leaders, we had to act to protect those rights. Indeed, the right of self-determination was more of a concern to us than whether workers would choose unionization if it came down to a vote.

Yet when we looked at the press coverage of the New Haven fight and other corporate campaign battles, we understood that the hospitals had had a very difficult time presenting themselves in a good light and generating political and community support. For a hospital that had just come through a bruising financial crisis and had finally found its feet, a public attack on our reputation could have been deadly. Such exposure would carry a real setback risk in terms of physician recruitment, referrals from community doctors, and, ultimately, finances.

Some observers suggested that we engage in a traditional media campaign. One well known Boston media consultant said:

> The best press strategy, I think, is three-fold.
>
> First, the light of day helps you. Ask for a *mano a mano* public event that allows Paul to debate the facts directly with the Union, so he can respond to misinformation/ disinformation being fed to the media and their members. Perhaps a Commonwealth Magazine sponsored debate/ forum would work.
>
> Second, either a 'big' Boston Magazine/Boston Globe Magazine article needs to be written which allows for an airing of both sides of the 'arguments,' with the writer arbitrating the 'truth' from the hyperbole.
>
> Finally, BIDMC needs to 'adopt' one long term media ally that you can call on each time you need an immediate 'pushback' story. Candidates include [names omitted]. All

are smart, independent, and willing and able to take in and understand complex issues and then try write about them in a way that will be interesting and understandable to the public and opinion leaders. They all know and like Paul, but are ignorant to the differences in the competing arguments.

One of my internal advisors realized this approach was ill-conceived:

> Interesting but wrong on all counts, I think: gives the union a forum, standing and legitimacy that it currently lacks; empowers the print media as arbiters, while their influence declines almost daily; the third point is objectionable on its face. [Name] thinks of this as fundamentally a media issue – but it isn't, it's a leadership issue here. No one can force us to rollover to union demands but us.

I relied on this view and that of one of my most trusted personal advisors, Monique Doyle Spencer. Monique was an experienced public relations professional in Boston. She warned me:

> Well, if there will be a battle, it may as well be bruising, and it usually goes better if you come out swinging. The interesting thing about this battle to me is that there will be many different fields. It used to be that you fought it out in the *Globe* and maybe TV picked it up. But now there will be blogs and there will be all those inexperienced reporters at the TV stations who know nothing about Boston or labor. You're going to need to play this both in public, on the Internet and with the employees.

I realized, therefore, that I needed a medium that could tell the story of the corporate campaign in a compelling manner. I needed people to understand that the campaign was simply a technique for undermining the democratic principles behind a union certification election. The narrative had to be that this was not a matter of whether or not our hospital should have a union. It was a matter of allowing free and fair debate among workers and between workers and supervisors as part of an election process, something not possible with a neutrality agreement. It was a matter of ensuring the sanctity of a secret ballot, something not possible with a card check process.

I needed a medium that would undercut the effectiveness of the "thousand cuts" that would be coming our way from the SEIU. I knew that the union would use all kinds of traditional communication vehicles: Purchased ads in newspaper, television, radio, and public transit. I also knew that it would employ blog sites, email, and the like to reach the growing number of people using social media. My approach, though, would have to be based on an extremely limited budget. It would have to be nimble and quickly responsive. It should not be filtered by reporters and editors. In addition, it should be free.

I needed a medium, too, that would reach and persuade a variety of important constituencies--the workers in our hospital, the trustees, public officials, and the press--that the traditional form of union elections was consistent with the democratic principles of all elections. In negotiation parlance, I needed a medium that would preclude the SEIU from degrading our alternatives and might even enhance them.

The answer was a blog. In August of 2006, I had started to write a blog entitled "Running a Hospital," for the purpose of presenting stories and discussions about a range of issues relating to health care and medicine. Because it was unusual for a hospital CEO to have a personal blog, it was widely read in the Boston area, both by workers in the hospital and by outside observers. The *Boston Globe* considered the existence of the blog newsworthy enough to include a story about it in the business section of the newspaper, further enhancing its outreach. The major consumer health care advocacy organization in Boston, Health Care for All, likewise helped spread the word.[xviii]

I was careful to maintain high standards for my blog, knowing that it was important to maintain my credibility. I tried to write well and clearly about a variety of health care issues. All posts were written by me alone, with no input from or review by the hospital's public affairs or legal departments, so that they would be spontaneous and unbureaucratic and have a consistent "voice." In addition to discussing public policy issues, I related many sad, happy, and dramatic stories about our doctors, nurses, and other staff as they pursued their dedicated work in our clinical settings. I allowed anyone to comment on my blog – anonymous or not – and treated commenters respectfully. By October of 2006, my approach was paying dividends. Indeed, the blog succeeded beyond my wildest dreams in sparking thoughtful discussion and debate on many subjects. I could tell from my blog statistics that reporters for the city's major media outlets were regular readers, as were politicians and appointed government leaders.[xix] A trusted advisor wrote:

> I think that what is most successful has been the ability to create a high level of discourse on the blog. By getting out of the gate quickly, establishing yourself as a thought leader, and establishing a thoughtful cadre of readers, you have begun to inoculate yourself against negative posts, as they will appear somewhat out of place.

The blog served as an important enhancement to traditional media methods. Unlike like op-eds, which are subject to approval and editing by newspaper editors, I could write and publish my posts quickly, using the phrasing of my choice. Unlike newspaper stories, there was no need to convince a reporter or editor of the newsworthiness of a given story idea or compete with the other news of the day. If I felt a story was ripe, it could be posted on my blog for the world to see in a matter of minutes. By linking my blog to publish simultaneously on my Facebook and Twitter accounts, I could leverage my work, as thousands more readers would view my article in real time. Also, I didn't need to worry about being misquoted or misunderstood or having an inappropriate headline.

Overall Strategy: Expose the playbook

Having in hand a no-cost, credible, widely read, and flexible medium, I decided to use the blog to expose the SEIU's corporate campaign playbook.

First, though, I needed to set forth the set of principles that would guide our hospital in its labor relations. After all, you can't just complain about the other side's tactics: You need to demonstrate that your own stance is consistent with fundamental American values of fairness. I presented this exposition in my earliest posts and continued to reinforce it over the years. By repeating the text of emails I had sent to my staff, I explained to my readers how a neutrality agreement or card-check would violate those principles and why we could not compromise on such matters. Here is one of those messages, first sent to the staff and then posted publicly on the blog in August 2006:[xx]

> The other major change in the local environment is the announcement by a national union that it intends to organize the workers in the academic medical centers in Boston. I want to make our position clear with regard to this effort and union organizing efforts in general. We intend to follow the law with regard to labor relations, a law that is designed to give a fair opportunity both to employees who favor unionization and those who oppose it. Congress has been very clear that employers have to give workers a fair choice in these matters. Accordingly, we will vigorously oppose any efforts to short-circuit the

legitimate process by which employees of this hospital can consider, debate, and vote on this issue. For me the underlying question is whether a union at BIDMC would enhance your ability to deliver the kind of patient care that is so important to all of us, to strengthen our research program, to improve our education programs, to strengthen our ability to serve the community, and to improve our employees' chances for personal and professional development and advancement. I do not believe that it would, and so I intend to advise you against creating a union here. Ultimately, though, the choice will be yours, and we will respect your judgment on that matter if and when the time comes for a fair and free vote on this issue.

Having set this stage, I then used this post to explain, both to our internal and external audiences, the nature of a corporate campaign and how it was designed to overturn these basic principles of fairness. It was a message I would repeat many times during the following years:

> My belief is that a topic as important as unionization deserves a free exchange of views. If the management of the hospital agrees to a "neutrality" agreement that limits our ability to discuss the pros and cons of the issue, that would be at variance with the history and culture of this academic medical center, a tradition steeped in open dialogue and exchange of views.
>
> Let me say again: We believe in free elections in which each employee, unencumbered by peer pressure or other outside forces, gets to vote "yes" or "no" in the sanctity of

a private voting place. Thus, we cannot agree to a "neutrality" agreement nor to a system that bypasses the federal NLRB election process.

In other parts of the country, hospitals that have taken similar positions to ours have found themselves subject to massive public relations attack by unions. The object of these attacks seems to be to denigrate the reputation of the hospitals and to put pressure on volunteer boards of trustees and management to agree to the unions' organizing terms.

We hope and trust that the SEIU will not use these tactics in Boston. It is hard for us to imagine that a union that says that it is dedicated to improving the healthcare system would intentionally undermine public confidence in one of the world's best hospitals. But this has happened elsewhere, so we must be prepared for that eventuality. We will hold fast to our principles and would participate in a union organizing process based on the rules and regulations set forth in federal law, a process designed to protect the rights of all parties. We have too much respect for our employees to bargain away your rights to a free and fair election. We trust the people who work here, and we would respect your judgment should an election be authorized. You earn that trust every day by the way you take care of patients, participate in research, train medical professionals and one another, and support a wide variety of community activities.

As time went by, I carefully set forth the details of the "playbook" that the SEIU would use in a corporate campaign against us. Sure enough, the union began to follow that expected set of measures in order, giving me further ammunition to write blog posts confirming my predictions. Here is one from July 2007, after the union started to spread false stories that our financial audit had misrepresented the amount of charity care our hospital had provided and threatened to seek a review by the state legislature:[xxi]

> Here's how it works in detail. Any hospital the size of BIDMC ($1 billion in revenues, hundreds of thousands of patients, millions of square feet of space) files tons of documents with federal, state, and local regulatory agencies. The union hires several dozen bright, committed young researchers and tells them to scour every line and item in all these reports. You look for inconsistencies, ambiguities, and patterns, and then you issue a public report stating that the hospital was incorrect in the handling of a certain matter or knowingly misrepresented some issue or other. You also ask for a review of the matter by a legislative committee.
>
> The key is to pick a topic that garners a headline and public concern, like provision of care to poor people. It is also helpful to pick an arcane accounting issue that few understand, so that a cogent and concise rebuttal by the hospital is virtually impossible in the regular media.
>
> The next page in the playbook is an important intermediate step. You send letters to the homes of the hospital's board of trustees asserting that they are not carrying out

their fiduciary responsibilities in properly supervising the management on the matters raised. Later – if there is no response or if you don't find the answer fully responsive – you publicly assert that the hospital's board is not sufficiently diligent about those responsibilities.

And what if the patient stories are exaggerated or untrue? Well, since a hospital is not allowed to discuss individual patient cases under HIPAA or state law or under the hospital's quality assurance peer review process, it would be left to give a general response that will not appear persuasive in the public eye.

Meanwhile, using the blog, I continued to elucidate our hospital's principles on labor relations issues, principles that were consistent with the law but also tied to the purpose and ethical standards of our institution. For example, in September 2007, I posted our board-approved Code of Conduct. The prologue: [xxii]

> BIDMC has a strong commitment to its mission of community service in providing excellent clinical care, conducting medical research, and training future generations of medical professionals. As an academic medical center and prominent member of the corporate and civic communities, BIDMC is committed to an environment of respectful and open discourse and debate among its management, employees and physicians. It is of the utmost concern to the Board of Directors that this fair and unhindered exchange of points of view is maintained and supported during all times, including any attempt by

unions to organize staff at BIDMC. Therefore the Board of Directors adopts this General Code of Conduct.

The blog post included the entire Code of Conduct, including the portion carefully written to contrast with the undemocratic purposes of a neutrality agreement:

> When communicating with employees, including regarding union activities, managers and supervisors are encouraged to promote an open and robust dialogue and share with employees factual information. Managers and supervisors also should feel free to express their opinions and encourage employees to ask questions. On the other hand, in any discussions with employees, respect is paramount. Specifically in the union activities context, managers and supervisors must not threaten or interrogate employees about their union activities, nor may managers or supervisors make promises to employees to induce them to be against the union. Finally, managers and supervisors must not conduct surveillance of union activities.

I was careful to stick to principles and facts in my blog posts. While I sometimes poked fun at the union's tactics,[xxiii] I never engaged in name-calling or aspersions about its staff or motives. I never questioned whether its underlying mission or concern for workers was genuine. However, as in the sentences above, I also referred to the union as "it," rather than "they." This was meant to underscore the corporate and impersonal nature of the SEIU, as differentiated from the kind and well-intentioned people working in our hospital.

The blog served to undercut many of the SEIU's tactics by creating a context for those tactics with journalists. Very often, when the union would issue a press release on one of its claims, the assigned reporter would call us and ask, "Is this another part of their corporate campaign?" When this point was confirmed, the reporter would either choose not to cover the story at all or to bury it deep in the paper as a small item. A key element of the corporate campaign communications strategy was thereby eviscerated. But we still had to deal with mitigating the union's tenacity in persuading a number of targeted constituencies of the corporate campaign. Let's turn now to several of those battlefields.

CHAPTER 3

Fronts in the War

The first battlefield:
Neutralize use of the religion card

The SEIU has often employed religion in its corporate campaigns, and this was one of the earliest tactics used against BIDMC. Part of this approach is to appeal to members of a religious community that might be affiliated with the institution to put pressure on the management.[xxiv] The "BI" in BIDMC stands for "Beth Israel," and the hospital was established by the Jewish community in the early 1900s. Also, I happened to be a Jewish CEO of the hospital. As Jews have had a long history of pro-union advocacy, the SEIU spared no effort to try to garner support from union supporters in the Jewish community. All of a sudden, people from my faith, who had not been in touch for years or who were connected to me only by two or three degrees of separation, would show up to have a private conversation. A childhood friend living in Boston, whom I had barely seen since our days in Hebrew school, sent me a note out of the blue. He said:

> I was concerned for you to be in a potentially very difficult fight and what that would mean for you and for BI. I was also concerned because I know something of some of the people involved in the union and I don't think they're all one dimensional people you would never want to work with. I know you have to make your own decision, but I'm just interested in trying to talk with you because of how long I've known you and my feeling that at our age life is short and there are more questions now about legacy.

I was personally offended by this tactic but more importantly felt that shining a light on these conversations must be an important part of my blog's counter-campaign. I addressed these issues head-on first in October 2006: [xxv]

> Recently, a person affiliated with unions in Massachusetts said to me, "As one Jew to another, I would hate to think that you would be publicly taking the kind of position you have been taking on this SEIU matter." I was really stunned by this--to think that this issue would be couched as a matter of religion, rather than being addressed on the merits. My response to him was, "As one Jew to another, I would like to think that you would be ashamed of me if I did not stand up to an undemocratic approach that undercut the rights of a group of people."

See the posting below on union activities for background on this issue, and then answer the question: What do you think? Was he out of line? Am I?

One of the first comments posted by a reader helped make the case:

> Wow! Yes, I think he was totally out of line. And somewhat incomprehensible. What does being a Jew have to do with union organizing? What was his point? I think your comments have been totally fair, balanced, sensible and unemotional. Everything the situation calls for. BID employees are lucky to have you as their leader and, as a member of the community, I feel confident that whatever the outcome, it will truly be the wish of the majority of BID's employees. As it should be!

I kept up the theme in a more indirect way in December 2008, after the SEIU had started to purchase billboards and created a website called "Eye-on-BI."[xxvi] Its ads again made not-so-subtle mention of the Jewish heritage of Beth Israel Deaconess Medical Center. Many employees found this offensive, and I used the opportunity to publish an email I had received from one, Michael Scanlon:[xxvii]

> The billboards I have seen cast aspersions on the hospital that I know to be false and inappropriate from my personal experience. After some exploration I discover that this is an attempt to unionize the hospital, but the advertising does not say anything obvious about that issue.

Questions such as who it is that wants to unionize, what group they represent, what ills might result from the lack of unions, or what dialogue is taking place between the unions and the hospital administration are not raised by the advertising.

I can see no constructive agenda which approaches the issue of unionization, and as an observer on the street I don't even know who is making these accusations or why. Add to these facts that it is only the "Jewish" hospital that is being targeted and the only conclusion I can draw is that even if this group is trying to accomplish something valid it is playing subtly on age old prejudices about Jews and money rather than presenting their position in a cogent and fair manner. This is very destructive and insults the good intentions of labor as a movement in general – a movement deeply indebted to Jews, by the way.

I have personalized this because unlike the folks running the "Eye on the BI campaign" I want you to know exactly what my agenda is. I am a sixty-year-old Christian who has nursed a partner through death from AIDS and been saved from the same fate at the Beth Israel Deaconess Medical Center over the last few years. I am angered by the "Eye on the B.I." campaign not just because they attack an institution to which I owe my life, but because they are doing it in an underhanded, destructive, and malicious way.

The religious part of the SEIU campaign had several dimensions. In November 2007, an op-ed showed up in the local Jewish newspaper:

Today, tens of thousands of residents of Greater Boston are working day in and day out to make ends meet, often at more than one job, and often with very limited benefit packages. Many of those workers are employees of the excellent teaching hospitals that provide so much of our region's health care and drive such a large portion of our local economy. And as of a year ago, 1199SEIU – the health care workers' union – has been trying to organize many of those workers, including those at Beth Israel-Deaconess Medical Center.

Now come back to today and SEIU's organizing efforts here in Boston–and learn that Paul Levy, the President of BIDMC, has made clear he wants no union at his hospital. Mr. Levy is of course entitled to his opinion, but what disappoints me most is not Mr. Levy's statements–bosses discouraging workers from unionizing is nothing new in American history–but rather the silence on the part of the organized Jewish community in response.

Do we not still believe that working people deserve an organized and unified voice on the job? Do we not still believe that the unions that benefited our grandparents and our parents should benefit this generation of workers? And now that so many of us are professionals–with many of us running the biggest economic institutions in Boston– do we not still believe it is our responsibility to continue to work for social justice?

I want to put out a call to our community's business leaders, and direct it first to Beth-Israel's President: Mr. Levy, you are using your powerful position to stop workers from organizing. You can call it your First Amendment right to speak out, or your duty to your hospital, but your aggressive speech will silence others less powerful than yourself.

Knowing that this newspaper had widespread circulation among the Jewish community, I needed to quickly set the record straight. I asked the editor for equal space, and he granted it to me. Knowing that I could only include a small number of words, I linked the article to the more extensive expositions on the blog. Consistent with our themes, I entitled the op-ed "Open Discourse on Union Issues":

> A column last week by Ben Healey accuses me of "aggressive speech" with regard to the question of whether people at Beth Israel Deaconess Medical Center should choose to create a union to represent them. Mr. Healey frames the issue of unionization in the context of the Jewish tradition of social justice.
>
> Here is what I have actually said on this topic, so you can decide whether it is "aggressive" and whether what I have said is in any way inconsistent with the teachings of our faith. Here are the words I used in an email message to our staff in October 2005:
>
> "I want to make our position clear with regard to this [SEIU organizing] effort and union organizing efforts in general. We intend to follow the law with regard to labor relations, a law that is designed to give a fair opportunity both to employees who favor unionization and those who oppose it. Congress has been very clear that employers

have to give workers a fair choice in these matters. Accordingly, we will vigorously oppose any efforts to short-circuit the legitimate process by which employees of this hospital can consider, debate, and vote on this issue. For me the underlying question is whether a union at BIDMC would enhance your ability to deliver the kind of patient care that is so important to all of us, to strengthen our research program, to improve our education programs, to strengthen our ability to serve the community, and to improve our employees' chances for personal and professional development and advancement. I do not believe that it would, and so I intend to advise you against creating a union here. Ultimately, though, the choice will be yours, and we will respect your judgment on that matter if and when the time comes for a fair and free vote on this issue."

The SEIU has recently asked the Boston hospitals to agree to organizing rules that would limit free and open debate on this matter. No major Boston hospital has agreed to these terms. In contrast, our Board of Directors has adopted a code of conduct around this issue that is fully consistent with federal law and regulations. Here is an excerpt:

"When communicating with employees, including regarding union activities, managers and supervisors are encouraged to promote an open and robust dialogue and share with employees factual information. Managers and supervisors also should feel free to express their opinions and encourage employees to ask questions. On the other hand, in any discussions with employees, respect is paramount. Specifically in the union activities context, managers and supervisors must not threaten or interrogate employees about their union activities, nor may managers or supervisors make promises to employees to induce them to be against the union. Finally, managers and supervisors must not conduct surveillance of union activities."

Does any of this sound aggressive or inconsistent with traditions of social justice? For more of my opinion on these matters, please check my blog [link included].

A month later, the newspaper permitted the author to have space for another piece, and I quickly sent a follow-up note to the editor:

Again, you have published an opinion piece from Mr. Healy that is inaccurate with regard to our hospital and me personally.

Is it your preference that he and I continue to engage in back-and-forth op-eds on this subject? I am pleased to do so if you think it would be of interest to your readers. On the other hand, I am happy to respond with a short letter to the editor in response – but if you are going to continue to publish longer pieces from him on this topic, I feel compelled to ask you again for equal space, now and each time he does so.

He granted me leave to file a letter to the editor:

> To the editor,
>
> Mr. Healey's recent op-ed again mischaracterizes my statements concerning union activities. He refers to "my unilateral" code of conduct. This is not mine. It is United States labor law which gives both parties (the union and the employer) the right to voice its opinion concerning unionization. The union is trying to change the law so the employer will not have that right.
>
> Also, his comment that we ran "a scorched-earth campaign against skilled maintenance workers who were trying to form a union" a few years ago couldn't be further from the truth. Indeed, at the time, I wrote a letter to every person eligible to vote that said that we thanked everybody for an open, thoughtful debate on the questions involved and that, however the vote turned out, we would have a respectful and collegial relationship with all the staff.
>
> Mr. Healey's use of theological or other religious arguments is interesting. Perhaps his next op-ed will discuss his analysis of why the other major teaching hospitals in Boston have also not adopted the SEIU's proposed neutrality agreement. Most of their CEOs are Jewish, also.

That ended the issue at this newspaper.

The SEIU's use of religion as a tool sometimes led to ugly and insidious tactics. I did not always use the blog to respond to them. For example, employing one of the cruelest and most inappropriate techniques, the SEIU worked through a local Jewish Sunday school run by the Workmen's Circle. A colleague reported to me:

> My son and daughter-in-law attend Workmen's Circle programs and send their children to its Sunday school. The children mentioned that SEIU has been visiting the School, reporting that entry-level employees at BIDMC are "so poorly paid" that they "cannot afford health insurance." They are encouraging the children and others to stage a protest outside BIDMC this coming Sunday.
>
> My son and daughter-in-law are not subscribing to this, arguing that the School and others should hear both sides of the story and then decide for themselves wherein the facts lie. They have suggested that my grandson write a note to you asking if someone could come to the School to speak for BIDMC and, if so, urge that any decision re protest and public display be held off until that happens.

Notwithstanding this parental involvement, on a bitterly cold December day in 2007, fifth grade students were taken out to demonstrate and read letters they had written to hospital administrators urging them to allow union elections without interference. In a small story buried in the newspaper, the Boston Globe reported:[xxviii]

> "Every worker deserves to be treated fairly," 10-year-old Daavi Gazelle of Jamaica Plain told the crowd gathered on Brookline Avenue near Joslin Park. "This is not only in the interest of the workers, but the patients." The students and

their parents then chanted "Free and fair elections," drawing honks from passing drivers.

Lost in this slogan – "free and fair elections" – was the truth of the matter, that the SEIU's approach would actually undermine truly free and fair elections. I felt, though, that creating another public story about how these little children had been used would be cruel to them, in that I would have to publicly expose how they had been used by people they admired – their teachers and parents. (I do so now because the children are older and they and others deserve to know.) But I did ask the school administrators to permit me, in the tradition of Jewish debate and dialogue, to present the opposing point of view to the children. A board member at Workmen's Circle also asked on my behalf. The response was that the "curriculum" allotted only that brief time to labor issues of this sort, and they were now on to other matters.

This incident, however, did not go unnoticed. And, in the tradition of this religious community, it created a healthy debate among the Boston Jewish clergy leadership, many of whom had read my previous blog posts and the back-and-forth in the Jewish newspaper. One rabbi wrote to another:

> If you saw the letters that he received from their religious school children, I think that you'd agree that they are unethical, manipulative and shameful. Paul understood that he would be subjected to personal attack when he took the position that he has taken, but we ought to be

insistent (no matter where we stand on the labor issue) that certain tactics are reprehensible and unworthy of our support.

For the record, I have always been predisposed toward Union organizing, but I am aware, as you must be, that there are behaviors and misbehaviors that occur on both sides of the divide. I think that whenever we, as rabbis, support union causes, we also have an obligation to hold the unions to a high standard of ethical and moral behavior.

Shortly after this interplay, Jewish leadership involvement in the SEIU corporate campaign waned. I am not privy to all that went on among the rabbis, but I can only conclude that their long-standing sense of justice and fairness was disturbed by what had been going on. They understood that the values and principles to which I had personally and publicly committed our hospital were consistent with their own. I had helped create a context in which the SEIU's so-called faith-based positions were discredited. The union had overreached, offending the very constituency it was trying to secure. Its use of the religious card was ineffective and was quickly discarded as part of the corporate campaign.

The second battlefield: Keep the doctors on board

Meanwhile, back at the hospital, the SEIU corporate campaign went after two important constituency groups, our young doctors-in-training and our older attending physicians. This was not an issue of trying to unionize the doctors: The SEIU had no plans in that regard. Rather, the hope was to enlist them as advocates to create a divide between the medical staff and the hospital administration. At one point in May 2009, for example, the SEIU wrote to the residents in the hospital, asking them to fill out a survey. It contained a number of leading questions that were designed to provoke divisions.[xxix] Within hours, I posted the following thoughts on the blog:[xxx]

> This week, residents at our hospital received an email survey request from the SEIU. Does this mean the union is thinking about organizing the residents, or does it hope to obtain responses that would be helpful in a corporate campaign? Some residents wondered how SEIU has the resources to obtain their email addresses and also how it can afford to conduct this kind of survey.

Immediately, the social-media-literate residents started to post comments:

> Should I respond to this survey and tell them the truth, how enjoyable it truly is to work at BIDMC, how the salaries are fair for the market, and other generally positive things, or would they simply use this to twist any words I said to the negative?
>
> My gut tells me to toss the below e-mail in the garbage with an unsubscribe order, but my heart tells me to tell the positive truth.

> As a resident at BIDMC, I received the survey. It felt dirty just opening it. How on earth did they get my email? It's creepy and disturbing, just like this campaign against a hospital I love to work at.
>
> I took the survey. I think it has three purposes: to make residents think they are being treated unfairly; to make them feel nervous about budget cuts; to collect a number that says "employees at BID have no opportunity for salary talks." I often wonder how scummy people can stand going to work every day.
>
> What I find offensive is that they have a quotation from Dr. Martin Luther King, Jr., "1199 represents the conscience of the labor movement," on their web site, as if it is a justification for everything they do now.

And then there was this very dramatic comment from a resident who had started his training in another hospital:

> Prior to this institution, I had worked at an institution with SEIU, and I agree with the comment posted above by another former employee of a SEIU organization. The hospital was full of factions that fought each other on who had to do the work, not actually doing it. I frequently would hear "That ain't my job" (if I got a response at all) for simple things I needed done for a patient (or if they asked directly). And I got paid less and had to give dues to the union. The only thing I learned from that experience is that Unions only represent themselves. Unions only look out for themselves. They made sure they seemed important, but really did nothing of value. I thank my lucky

stars every day that I have been able to change my program to come to BIDMC, where people emphasize working together, where people do not think of what they have to do, but what they CAN do, regardless of their position to help the patients. And where everyone, from transporters to chiefs of departments work together as a family to come up with a solution to any problem that comes our way. For the first time in my short career, I feel supported in what I need to do to take care of patients. Shame on you, SEIU, for trying to take that away.

In a different era, the residents' comments to me would have been private, in a conversation or an email. But the blog permitted me to play them out to the entire BIDMC community, reinforcing their reactions among their colleagues – while also displaying them for the world at large.

The SEIU targeted the senior doctors, too, in a letter sent to the attending physicians in the hospital. Here is my post from January 2008, entitled ">500 letters in the mailroom," which included hyperlinks to previous posts about the corporate campaign:[xxxi]

> Our mailroom staff called today to say that over 500 letters had arrived from the SEIU to doctors in the hospital. One of the doctors was kind enough to share his with me, a letter from Mike Fadel, Executive Vice President. I'll spare you most of the details, but I will give you a small quote:

"BIDMC's CEO recently has complained that he has been singled out for public criticism on the 'question' of whether hospital workers should be promised that they will not be threatened by executives on the decision of unionizing. But he has singled out his own institution by essentially promising to fight against BIDMC's own caregivers as if they were adversaries."

Those of you who are regular readers of this blog know that all of the above is not true. You know the high regard and respect I have for our employees, and you know of my personal efforts to improve the work environment at this hospital- both for their sake and in support of providing better care to our patients. You can also see exactly what I have said [hyperlink here] about union organizing in general and the tactics of this union [hyperlink here] in particular.

The union's use of language is carefully chosen. It is meant, first, to isolate me by giving the impression that I am the only hospital CEO in Boston who feels this way. Not so. The others may not say so publicly, but they readily say so privately. (Who knows, perhaps they are wise to do it that way!)

Second, it is meant to try to create divisions between the doctors and the administration of the hospital. Not likely to be effective, either, in that the doctors see quite clearly what tactics are at play here.

I then returned to the union's use of the religion card:

A third subtle aspect of the package sent to the doctors is the inclusion of an op-ed from a Jewish newspaper that makes similar accusations and states that I am acting in a manner inconsistent with the "Jewish tradition of social justice." Months ago, I raised a hint [hyperlink here] as to this tactic as well. Perhaps the SEIU thinks that doctors at a hospital, one of whose antecedents was established by the Jewish community, would be receptive to this argument. Perhaps they don't understand that many people are likely to find it an offensive and mistaken use of religion in support of a political or organizational cause.

Meanwhile, I hear from friends on Beacon Hill that the union persists in complaining about this blog and what I say in it. What I say in it, as all of you know, is out there for the world to see and evaluate. If any of you catch me in a misleading comment or a mistake you can say so immediately and for the rest of the world to see.

Sunshine is the best disinfectant.

Again, the blog offered a timing advantage. I was able to distribute my response to the 500 letters even before the doctors had received them. I could thereby frame the SEIU message in its proper context. Here was a typical response:

> I just wanted to voice my personal support for your position. I am appalled by the scare tactics these unions use with people who may not be as well-read as others. If you ever want to circulate a support document for signatures, count me in – I'll sign it first.

One chief forwarded the blog to his faculty and told me:

> We tend to embrace these types of social issues; however, our faculty have the perspective of working with unionized nursing at [another Boston hospital]. We want what is best for our patients; these letters have absolutely had no traction in our department.

Although my public forum communications were proving effective, personal connection was still important. At least one department chief followed up with this note, asking me to come to his faculty meeting and discuss the situation with the doctors:

> Paul, I forwarded your blog to the department faculty, and one of them sent a "reply all" response talking to me but reaching the entire faculty, in which she presented a union-inspired response.
>
> I have a division heads meeting scheduled for this Wednesday at 10:45-12:00. I would appreciate it if you could attend, so that I can invite this person, and anyone else on the faculty who is interested to hear the hospital's side of the discussion. Would you be willing to do this? SEIU has clearly opened up a vein of support for themselves (we have a fair number of faculty who are old-line liberals who support labor), and these folks will respond to their message if we do not have a cogent (and rapid) answer.
>
> I have told the faculty that this is not a relationship of investors vs. workers, as it is in a usual union fight,

because BIDMC has no investors. Rather, we use every penny we get to improve patient care, and this is an issue of finding the balance between patient care and worker compensation. I think they will be receptive to that concept.

I mention this episode to illustrate that a blog, while a useful tool, is just one tool. Effective leadership cannot rely solely on electronic transmissions, a point I have noted in my previous book, *Goal Play! Leadership Lessons from the Soccer Field*:

> When John Maeda took on the job of President of the Rhode Island School of Design, he committed himself to an extraordinary amount of electronic communication with his community. But he found that this was not always the most effective way to proceed, as he notes in his book, Redesigning Leadership:
>
>> Traditional broadcast means of communicating, such ... as a campus-wide email, [are] sometimes necessary, but what I've become more and more enamored of is the simplicity of a conversation between two people. It is high-bandwidth, engaging, interactive, and, putting my fiscal hat on for a moment, "expensive." Yet, I've discovered it's the greatest tool that a leader really has.
>
> Much is made of a walking-around style of leadership, and there is a reason for that. Maeda quotes an interim head of RISD, Louis Fazzano: "It's the only way to feel the whole system ... and also to be felt."

The end result: The SEIU had absolutely no traction in enlisting attending physicians and residents in support of their proposals to modify the organizing process at BIDMC. An important constituency that the union was counting on to put pressure on the management and board was removed from the equation.

The third battlefield: Engage the staff

Of course, the hospital workers, as those who would become future union members, were the SEIU's essential constituency to convince. Here, the union provided me with a wonderful opportunity: It was so focused on following its playbook that the organizers spent virtually no time at all bothering to get to know workers personally and finding out their concerns.[xxxii] The workers' image of the SEIU, then, was mainly formed by two vehicles: the SEIU's advertisements and my blog. Both worked to the SEIU's disadvantage.

One of the less thought-out aspects of a corporate campaign that seeks to denigrate an institution is that the disparagement tends to spill over as an attack on the people working within that organization, creating anger and resentment. The blog was useful in helping the hospital staff see that the SEIU's attacks on the hospital were, in essence, attacks on their own dedication and professionalism. In September 2008, I posted a column entitled "Corporate Campaign – The Next Chapter." Highlights:[xxxiii]

Many of you have sent me notes during the last few days expressing your dismay at the negative advertising and other activities being carried out by the Service Employees International Union (SEIU). I thought I would take a moment to put this all in context.

We live in a free country, where people and organizations are free to say pretty much anything they want in public media. Thus, SEIU can say and imply a lot. But, saying these things is not the same as being truthful in what it is saying.

It is clear that SEIU is engaged in what is called a "corporate campaign," an attempt to harm the reputation of our hospital and denigrate the people working or volunteering here. Another goal of such a campaign is to isolate us and to turn our closest friends against us. Why would the union do this? Well, its goal is to put such enormous pressure on the management and the Board of Directors that we agree to concessions that would make it more likely for the union to be successful when it gets to the point of trying to organize workers in this hospital. It wants us to sign a contract—negotiated only between management and high-level union leaders—that would govern the union organizing process and would rob our employees of their right to a vigorous and open debate prior to a meaningful secret ballot election.

Now, we see real evidence of this corporate campaign. SEIU is spending thousands and thousands of dollars on mobile billboards, bus stop ads, newspaper ads, and ads on expensive radio stations to get across its current messages.

We do not have access to union dues, nor do we currently choose to spend our funds to counter these types of ads in the public media, and so it will likely feel unfair to you that the union's charges go unanswered in those forums.

I do not feel it is productive or a good use of time to try to rebut each and every charge made by the SEIU. But, you should rest assured that any and all complaints and allegations raised with regard to issues like our rates, our delivery of charity care, human resources policies and individual cases are governed by a variety of state and federal regulatory agencies. The public will know through these agencies when we make a mistake. But as you well know, our hospital is committed to levels of transparency that are unprecedented in the Boston area. For example, we even publicized when we made a serious medical error so that we could engage in a constant process of improvement on behalf of our patients!

Instead of recognizing our good intentions, our attributes and our initiatives on behalf of patients and employees, SEIU seeks to muddy our reputation with inaccurate and exaggerated claims. That it chooses to do so mainly with regard to BIDMC rather than other hospitals in Boston may be a direct result of my decision to call out its strategies and behavior in a public way, for example on my blog and in public appearances. I felt it important to do so to inform public officials, the media, and corporate leaders on this important matter. I believe many CEO colleagues in other Massachusetts hospitals agree with me, but they have chosen to be quiet about the issue, probably in the hope of not being targeted by the union. I believe that is a mistake on their part, in that they will likely be next in line, as the president of SEIU has said that the union will not rest until every hospital worker in Boston is unionized.

I know that for some of you it is difficult to be placed in the middle of this campaign. The union may say that it has no intention of harming you personally, but you understand that it is the people who make a hospital, and that nasty statements about the hospital are, in essence, an attack on you personally. I am sorry that this is the case. All I can say is that, while the ads and allegations can be upsetting, you should continue to be proud of your commitment and dedication to our mission of quality care and compassion for those in need. That mission continues unabated and strong, even in the face of these terribly misleading ads. Thank you for all that you do. As always, I am happy to hear from you individually if you want to share your personal concerns and suggestions.

The response from the staff was overwhelming, both in the form of comments on the blog and in emails to me. Strikingly, even on the blog, where anonymous comments were permitted, people would sign their names. This was clearly a case in which people wanted their colleagues to know where they stood! Here are a few samples:

> *Ann:* I am very proud of the work I do here at BIDMC and I am thrilled to be employed in a hospital that doesn't incorporate the SEIU. If they were in this hospital it would

be less of a place in my opinion. You so well put it into perspective and that is always comforting. BIDMC is a wonderful institution and does not deserve the untruthful maligning that is the product of the SEIU, they absolutely disgust me in their conduct. The media should be vetting their business practices and unethical tactics. You are supported in your efforts to set the record straight Paul, keep up the good work.

Douglas: I have been contacted, via unsolicited mailings, from this union and read the terrible things they've chosen to print in various publications. I know that these half-truths are meant to harm the medical center's reputation. I understand that to them, BI represents a lot of money in member dues and that these tactics are meant to be divisive and hurt morale of our staff so they can swell their ranks and coffers. Staffs are often enticed by the "grass is greener" argument to join a union. I know from personal experience that this simply isn't true and that unions today do not improve quality, efficiency, or employee relations. I have no respect for their underhanded tactics. Please continue to fight the underhanded tactics and lies of this self-serving, power-hungry group. You have our support.

Judi: The SEIU's tactics and mistruths are shameful. Many have expressed anger that their campaigns are so insulting to our BIDMC family and do take it personally!

Marion: I heard an ad on the radio on my way home from work yesterday and I was shocked, I almost stopped the car to pay attention more closely. When I heard who had paid for the radio spot it all made sense. I hope that others will see through the message when they realize who is the messenger. Shameful!

Romy: Thank you so much for sending this email. I've been at the BI for over 6 years and started off as a travel-nurse. I had enough confidence in the establishment to sign on as a staff nurse and would never think of moving to another hospital. I believe in our practice, mission and values. I understand the concept of free speech, but it certainly hits a sensitive spot when people purposely set out to mar reputations through smear campaigns. I appreciate you giving some feedback on this matter. This solidifies my faith in this hospital.

Juliana: It is very comforting to read his article, as it soothes the anger on reading such untruths written and advertised by this union. To them I say evil does not harm good, ever. Through my almost 30 years of working at the BIDMC, I have never been treated unfairly in any way. Trying to disgrace the BIDMC IS NOT THE WAY TO WIN OVER UNION MEMBERS.

I received these kinds of responses regularly during the years that the SEIU was engaged in its corporate campaign. Of course, I also published contrary comments, but they were always posted anonymously and were obviously written by union organizers. The blog made evident the union's strategic blunder in trying to undermine the sense of mission and purpose of the hospital, as it offered the opportunity for staff members to respond publicly to the perceived insults. Absent the blog, the union's attacks could well have created a sense of unease and discomfort for the staff, but they would have been alone in that discomfort. Instead, they now faced a common enemy with the energy of a united team under a leader who would stand by them and stand for them. Thus, the staff-focused element of the union's corporate campaign was driven to utter failure. The union lost support among the very workers it might someday seek to organize.

The fourth battlefield:
Engage and reassure the affiliate

A corporate campaign often is designed to spill over to affiliated institutions of the target organization. The idea is to make those affiliates feel uncomfortable in their relationship with the owner, again to put pressure on the owner's management to give in on organizing principles. The SEIU tried to put pressure on BIDMC through activities affecting our small affiliated community hospital, BID Hospital~Needham, but I was able to use the blog to remind the workers and governing body and community members in Needham that the SEIU was engaging in tactics that were counter to their interests. At the time, BID~Needham was engaged in a $28 million dollar expansion and improvement project–supported in great measure by funds from our large downtown hospital—including a 37,000-square-foot addition that would double the size of the crowded emergency room and also add much needed in-patient beds.

On October 25, 2008, the SEIU showed up at a fundraiser for this project with a mobile billboard truck to publicize its campaign against BIDMC. I took a picture of the truck and on the next day, I wrote:[xxxiv]

> The picture above is of the mobile billboard hired by the SEIU to publicize its "Eye on BI" campaign. The union sent it to be visible at a fund-raising event held Friday night for our affiliated community hospital, BID~Needham.
>
> Let's think about this. The attendees at this event are loyal supporters of this community hospital. They serve as voluntary members of its governing bodies, and they donate their hard-earned money to the hospital because they believe in its mission and have confidence in the management and staff. They know that SEIU opposed the issuance of bonds to finance the expansion of the hospital's emergency room and other services. They come out for a pleasant evening together to support the hospital, and they see the SEIU spending money on a mobile billboard to denigrate the reputation of the academic medical center that has also provided millions of dollars in support of their community hospital.
>
> (In case you are wondering, a mobile billboard like this can be purchased for stints of 220 hours of travel time. The rental cost is $12,100 per 220 hours. There is also a $3,500 production fee for the panels.)

Is this effective? Well, you can be sure that attendees at this gathering were not impressed and remain very loyal to the institution.

I also issued a follow-up in April 2009, as the expansion project was reaching its successful conclusion:[xxxv]

> As noted by one of our staff: "In a period of five years the emergency room went from 9,500 patients to over 14,000," she said. "It's not just a town hospital anymore. We've expanded services, we've seen a growth in the town and the communities around us and people are getting to know us better."
>
> Regular readers will recall that this expansion and the bonds to finance it were opposed by SEIU, both at the town planning board and in front of MA HEFA, one of the designated public agencies for coordinating the issuance of tax-exempt bonds by schools, hospitals, and other non-profit entities in the state. Fortunately, the highly professional staff and board at MA HEFA found no merit in SEIU's arguments.

The SEIU totally misread the sentiments of the BID~Needham board members, staff, and community. Helped along by the blog, those constituencies came to understand our opposition to the union's tactics and its proposals to revamp the organizing process. They were offended by the spillover of the corporate campaign to their community and never once suggested to the management or board of BIMDC that we should retreat from our position on an appropriate unionization process. Quite the contrary: They often urged us to hold firm.

**The fifth battlefield:
Involve the governing bodies**

BIDMC had three levels of governing boards: an 18-member board of directors, which held the fiduciary authority for the institution; a 40-member board of trustees, which carried out the day-to-day governing committee work of the organization; and a 150-member board of overseers, loyal supporters of the hospital from the community. Recall that the purpose of a corporate campaign is to denigrate the reputation of the hospital and thereby create embarrassment and discomfort for board members. The hoped-for goal is to have those lay leaders put pressure on the management to "take the heat off" by agreeing to a card-check or neutrality agreement. Once that happens, unionization is virtually assured.

While we conducted a short educational program for the board members as to the nature of this campaign and what to expect, most of them had not lived through a comparable situation. We needed them to be alert to the progress of the corporate campaign and events so they would feel comfortable talking about them not only among themselves but also with their friends and colleagues in the community. After all, one corporate campaign technique is for board members of the targeted institution to hear from their respected peers in the community raising issues and doubts.

While I could have engaged with board members in regular emails, I felt that those would likely prove tiresome and annoying over time and might lose effectiveness. Again, the blog proved useful. Many of the board members were regular readers of my blog. For those who were not, when something significant occurred, I could send a simple note with a link to the latest blog post. The board members, in turn, could share the link with colleagues in their business and social circles. Everyone – inside and outside of the organization – would thereby get the same message.

Here, too, the blog succeeded in neutralizing the corporate campaign. I'll share with you just three of the many comments I received over the years from board members:

> *From an overseer:* I love these excerpts from your blog. When confronted with a bully, you have two choices – run or confront and risk having the snot beaten out of you.
>
> This far and no farther. The line has to be drawn by good people of conscience, and you are doing it with complete transparency by giving the bully equal time on your turf, exposing him with his own words and reasonably, rationally addressing the charges in a very public forum and identifying the tactics for what they are. You are excellent at not letting the baiters skew your commentary to being any-

thing about unions but rather the unconscionable tactics being used by a new bully under the guise of the right of workers to unionize.

From a trustee: I spent about ten years in labor negotiations taking point for two different companies. We decertified a union, drove back an organization drive, and had a strike. I wish I had you in my corner; or, was able to follow your blog for inspiration or as a blueprint to communicate openly with all. Your blog is out there for all to read. This is no shadowy smear campaign. A good and open communicator like you is very threatening to SEIU. This will be studied in years to come as another case study in labor/management relations. As a patient, an insurance paying employer, a taxpayer, a member of the greater Boston community and a trustee of the medical center, thank you.

From a director (after a particular blog post): One of your best! I think that the more that people can read what is factually going on the better chance we'll have that our employees will see the light. This will be a long battle, but I am proud of how you are and have taken it on.

The result: The union's corporate campaign failed at its core mission, to provoke pressure on management from the governing bodies. Never once during my tenure as CEO did any board member suggest to me that we accede to the SEIU's demand for a neutrality agreement or for a card-check form of organizing.

The sixth battlefield: Convey the story to the state legislature and Congress

The blog was also influential in the body politic. I knew from my readership statistics that it was regularly read by people on Beacon Hill and Capitol Hill. When the SEIU tried to stimulate government action by one or another "exposé," we often heard from elected officials privately, saying things like, "I can't afford to come out against them publicly, but I don't trust them either. I know what they are trying to do to you. You don't have to worry that people on Beacon Hill take seriously what they are saying about you."

The blog had a national audience as well, and may have had an effect on proposed legislation in the U.S. Congress. The union had introduced the so-called Employee Free Choice Act, which, if passed, would have mandated the card-check certification process whenever a union chose to use it. Right after the presidential election in 2008, I wrote:[xxxvi]

> With a new administration and Congress in place, we can expect a strong push for a new law that would eliminate secret ballot elections during certification drives by unions. This is the hallmark of efforts by the SEIU, which has received commitments from the President-elect and the Congressional Democrats that they will push this bill.

There is only one problem: Americans believe in secret ballot elections. Indeed, the one held on November 4 once again validates the importance of this great institution.

The SEIU and Democrats will try to brand Republicans as "anti-union" when they oppose this legislation. If the Republicans maintain a filibuster-proof minority in the Senate, the bill will not proceed. But even if the Democrats end up with 60 votes in the Senate, "blue dog" Democrats will not want their name attached to this bill in a roll-call vote on cloture.

One of the many tests facing the new President is whether he prefers to fight a combative battle on this issue – among all the others he is facing – or whether he will try an approach that brings people together.

And a similar question is whether Andy Stern, head of the SEIU, will acknowledge that Americans and their congressional representatives will be very uncomfortable with his proposal to eliminate elections and will say quietly to his friend the President-elect, "If you back off from your commitment to card-check as part of a bi-partisan deal, labor will still support you and the Congresspeople who vote with you."

Although supported by President Obama during his campaign and at the start of his term, the bill gradually died a slow death. There were many reasons why, but I heard from congressional staffers that our running commentary about the corporate campaign against a major teaching hospital partially undermined the SEIU's argument about the need for a change in the law. Once EFCA was clearly dead in Washington, the local SEIU organization understood that it was not politically attractive and totally dropped the card-check language it had been espousing in Boston.

On the personal side:
Prepare for the downside of speaking out

The one downside to my blog counter-campaign was the personalization of the union's campaign against me. I understood from the start that this was a likely outcome. After all, if I were successful in impeding its progress by exposing the playbook, the union would have to do its best to reduce that effectiveness by impeaching my character and even by trying to have me removed from the scene. Its website, "Eye on BI," became more and more targeted at me personally. Later, when I became involved in an embarrassing personnel issue, the union began to track my upcoming speaking engagements, looking for opportunities to trap or harass me.

An example occurred in May 2010, when I was scheduled to speak at a health quality conference in Ohio. I noticed that a large number of hits on my blog were originating from the SEIU office in that state, and so I knew that SEIU people would show up. With the union's help, a reporter from a Boston tabloid was advised of my speech and told of the plans to disrupt my talk. When she surprised me at Boston's Logan airport, she said that she was authorized to fly to Columbus to cover the speech but that "it would be better for me" if I agreed to talk to her in the gate waiting area. I did not, and she came along for the ride but was excluded by the conference organizers. Meanwhile, a member of the union slipped into the auditorium. Knowing this, I started my speech by mentioning the union's campaign and that they likely had people present. So, when the young man actually got up to ask his question, he was not able to be combative. Later, I noticed that he was holding a small tape recorder. Sure enough, the next edition of the tabloid had quotes from my speech, courtesy of the union representative who had given the tape recording to the reporter.

In a 2010 Labor Day interview, the newly appointed head of SEIU Local 1199, Veronica Turner, gave an interview to a local radio station in which she made clear the issue was personal and set forth her view of the future:[xxxvii]

> Mr. Levy stepped out on us. We did not go and start the fight with him. We would like for it not to be that way. But as long as he is leading that facility, I believe that it will be a fight.
>
> *Question:* Are you confident or not that you will be successful in organizing workers inside Beth Israel?
>
> *Answer:* I am overly confident.

The personal attacks continued. At the annual meeting of our hospital a few days later, a rolling billboard and several paid demonstrators showed up across the street. Both the billboard and the demonstrators' black t-shirts were emblazoned with the message "Fire Paul Levy!"

Before the meeting, our board chairperson had written this note to the governing boards:

> We have become aware of an advertising campaign sponsored by the SEIU ... attacking the governance of Beth Israel Deaconess Medical Center and urging us to fire Paul Levy. We are told they will run the ads heavily through Thursday evening, the night of our Annual Meeting.
>
> As you know, the BIDMC Board of Directors has completely reviewed all matters relating to Paul and has taken actions we believe are in the best interest of the medical center, including a unanimous conclusion that he is the person we want to continue to lead our hospital. So what is this ad campaign all about?
>
> It has been known for years that the SEIU has mounted a corporate campaign against BIDMC and the Board, in the hope that we will adopt procedures that would make it easier for them to unionize the hospital. This advertising campaign is just the latest step in their action plan. The SEIU is spending tens of thousands of dollars on TV, radio, print ads and billboards.
>
> The resolve of our board to do what is best for our patients and staff remains strong and will not be influenced by a high-cost advertising campaign.

At the annual meeting, far from being upset, our board members were amused. One of them went so far as to leave the room, go across the street, and ask a demonstrator if he could buy one of the t-shirts. The fellow said, "Just take one. I've got a lot in the truck." The board member presented it to me as a gift, saying, "Keep up the good work."[xxxviii]

CHAPTER 4

The result: A successful counter-campaign

The blog was successful in strengthening our hospital's internal and external communications and proved a potent weapon in counteracting the union's corporate campaign. During the entire campaign period from 2006 to 2011, there was no pressure on senior management from the BIDMC governing boards to negotiate a neutrality agreement, much less a card-check process. Press coverage of much of the union's campaign was neutralized. The union failed to gain the support of key external constituencies in both religious groups and the community at large. There was no sustained political support from key elected officials for such a negotiation. There was no groundswell of support from the hospital's residents, attending physicians, or workers to consider such an agreement. Further, the union never even tried to collect authorization cards. Outside of a few theatrical events at the hospital, its organizers were not seen on or near the campus.

While it was not possible to calculate the total number of dollars the union spent on its corporate campaign, we estimated it to be many hundreds of thousands of dollars. The expenses were all to no purpose, and I believe there was additional negative spillover for the union. During this time, the SEIU donated millions of dollars to political candidates in an attempt to place sympathizers in office. The union was generally unsuccessful, the clearest examples being the elections for U.S. Senator and for one Boston-area Congressman. Ultimately, too, the key organizer for the region was taken out of his position. It was later reported to me that people in the union viewed him as being overly aggressive with regard to our campaign, expending large sums of money with no documented results, except backlash against the union from workers and others loyal to the hospital.

I left the hospital in early 2011, after nine years in the job and for reasons unrelated to the SEIU, and am pleased to have kept the t-shirt presented to me by our board member. It is a reminder of the corporate campaign that the union had conducted for over five years, a campaign that resulted in no progress for its agenda. The SEIU had won neither a neutrality agreement nor a card-check process for organizing. The union had never even bothered to try to collect authorization cards for an election. Its contact with actual hospital workers, those who might be organized, was virtually a nullity. The lack of effectiveness in its expenditure of hundreds of thousands of dollars and hundreds of person-years of staff effort offers a lesson: In the new world of social media, the power of a well-funded corporate campaign can be diminished by a new generation of low-budget and highly flexible communication tools, available to any institution.

Note: I have created a website that has a compendium of all 51 of my SEIU-related blog posts from August 2006 through October 2010. You can find it at the following web address: http://exposingtheplaybook.com.

Endnotes

i http://www.boston.com/news/local/articles/2005/08/31/union_looks_to_organize_at_hubs_top_hospitals/

ii For example, respiratory therapists, radiology technicians, pharmacy technicians, medical equipment technicians, scrub nurses, transporters, secretaries, housekeepers, dietary workers, supply and inventory clerks and distributors.

iii Barry T. Hirsch and David A. Macpherson, "Union Membership and Coverage Database from the Current Population Survey: Note," Industrial and Labor Relations Review, Vol. 56, No. 2, January 2003, pp. 349-54. (in pdf); U.S. Bureau of Labor Statistics.

iv Matthew Kaminski, "Let's Share the Wealth," Wall Street Journal, December 6, 2008. http://online.wsj.com/article/SB122852244367484311.html

v http://runningahospital.blogspot.com/2009/02/is-this-free-part-or-fair-part.html

vi For example, 74% of eligible workers voted yes at one of the Caritas Christi hospitals. http://www.seiu.org/2009/10/nearly-600-ma-norwood-hositalworkers-vote-to-join-1199seiu.php

vii Manheim, Jarol B. *The Death of a Thousand Cuts: Corporate Campaigns and the Attack on the Corporation.* Lawrence Erlbaum Associates, Publishers. Mahwah, New Jersey. 2001. Page xiv.

viii Ibid. Page 120.

ix In 2007, the BNA reported: "The Service Employees International Union's recently launched 1-million-member health care union will have an annual budget of about $120 million and 4,000 organizers at its disposal to sign up the 10 million unorganized nonsupervisory health care workers in this country, its head said June 26." http://www.anh.com/ANHSnews/customer-files/NewSEIUHealthCareUnionWillHave120MillionBudget4000Organizers.pdf

x http://www.trusteemag.com/trusteemag_app/jsp/articledisplay.jsp?dcrpath=TRUSTEEMAG/PubsNewsArticleGen/data/2006NovDec/0611TRU_FEA_Union&domain=TRUSTEEMAG

xi http://www.chron.com/business/article/Public-pressure-is-key-in-union-manual-3832535.php

xii http://www.sutterhealth.org/about/labor/labor_1250-misinfo.html

xiii http://morethanmedicine.blogspot.com/2008/09/seius-corporate-campaign_12.html

xiv http://seiumonitor.com/wp-content/uploads/New-Haven-Register-11-30-04.pdf

[xv] http://seiumonitor.com/wp-content/uploads/New-Haven-Register-3-19-06.pdf
[xvi] Op cit. Page 271.
[xvii] Christopher Rowland, *Boston Globe*, "Hospitals expect hardball push to unionize." "Executives preparing to fight a powerful union that wants to organize workers at Boston teaching hospitals are studying how the union used an aggressive public relations campaign against Yale-New Haven Hospital in Connecticut." http://www.boston.com/business/healthcare/articles/2006/03/24/hospitals_expect_hardball_push_to_unionize/
[xviii] http://blog.hcfama.org/2006/09/26/paul-levy-joins-the-blogosphere/
[xix] The blog statistics program did not, of course, provide viewers' names, but it did provide their IP addresses.
[xx] http://runningahospital.blogspot.com/2006/08/union-issues.html
[xxi] http://runningahospital.blogspot.com/2007/07/pages-from-playbook.html
[xxii] http://runningahospital.blogspot.com/2007/09/another-page-from-playbook.html
[xxiii] Here's one where I "thanked" them for keeping mass transit fares lower by buying ads at transit stop kiosks: http://runningahospital.blogspot.com/2008/12/thanks-for-keeping-fares-down.html "Well, if in buying these local ads at 'T' stations, SEIU is helping to reduce the deficit of our transit system, I guess we should all be grateful!"
[xxiv] A story in the Los Angeles Times in 2005 documented other aspects of integrating religion into organizing campaigns, hiring "aspiring ministers, imams, priests and rabbis to spread the gospel of union organizing across the nation. "Stephanie Simon, "Labor and Religions Reunite." Los Angeles Times. July 17, 2005. http://articles.latimes.com/2005/jul/17/nation/na-union17/2
[xxv] http://runningahospital.blogspot.com/2006/10/religion-and-union-organizing.html
[xxvi] www.eyeonbi.org/
[xxvii] http://runningahospital.blogspot.com/2008/12/more-seriously-now.html
[xxviii] *Boston Globe*, "Youths lead union protest." December 3, 2007.
[xxix] For example: "Did BIDMC fairly compensate you for your residency? Did you have an opportunity to negotiate your salary and benefits?"
[xxx] http://runningahospital.blogspot.com/2009/05/seiu-surveys-residents.html
[xxxi] http://runningahospital.blogspot.com/2008/01/500-letters-in-mailroom.html
[xxxii] Contrast this with the highly personalized unionization campaign run by Kristine Rondeau and her colleagues at Harvard University. By the time of the NLRB vote, Kris and her colleagues had personally talked with virtually every possible member of the union. Hoerr, John. *We Can't Eat Prestige: the Women Who Organized Harvard*. Temple University Press, Philadelphia. 1977.
[xxxiii] http://runningahospital.blogspot.com/2008/10/corporate-campaign-next-chapter.html

xxxiv http://runningahospital.blogspot.com/2008/10/eye-on-sei.html
xxxv http://runningahospital.blogspot.com/2009/04/update-on-bidneedham-expansion.html
xxxvi http://runningahospital.blogspot.com/2008/11/next-step-for-labor-in-washington.html
xxxvii http://www.wbur.org/2010/09/06/seiu-boss, http://www.wbur.org/2010/09/06/seiu-boss/player
xxxviii The board member also asked the demonstrator if he was being paid to be there. "Of course. We all are," was the reply.